WORKBOOK

For

THE

SILVA MIND

CONTROL METHOD

A Practical Guide to

The Revolutionary Program by the Founder of the
World's Most Famous Mind Control Course

Michelle Danatwa Publishing

Disclaimer: The purpose of the exercises, questions, and content within this workbook is to enhance the reader's engagement with José Silva and Philip Miele's book, **"The Silva Mind Control Method: The Revolutionary Program by the Founder of the World's Most Famous Mind Control Course."** It is essential to recognize that this workbook serves as a complementary guide rather than the actual book itself. Authored independently and without the endorsement of José Silva and Philip Miele, it is a manifestation of deep admiration for his original work. Crafted with utmost respect, this workbook is designed as a valuable companion, offering readers a tool to comprehend and apply the profound ideas presented in the main book for enhanced understanding.

TABLE OF CONTENTS

How to Use this Workbook

Using this workbook for "The Silva Mind Control Method: The Revolutionary Program by the Founder of the World's Most Famous Mind Control Course" is like taking a special journey. First, think about what you want to achieve by using the workbook. Then, read the summary of important lessons from each chapter. After that, answer some questions to think deeply about what you've learned. Finally, do the exercises that go along with each chapter. You can also write down your own thoughts and ideas in the workbook. This workbook helps you understand the main book better and apply its lessons to your life. It's like a guide that helps you grow and learn more about yourself.

Overview of the Main Book

"The Silva Mind Control Method: The Revolutionary Program" by José Silva and Philip Miele presents a groundbreaking approach to harnessing the untapped potential of the human mind for personal growth and self-improvement. This seminal work introduces readers to the Silva Method, a comprehensive system of mental techniques and exercises designed to enhance cognitive abilities, foster self-awareness, and facilitate positive change.

At its core, the book explores the concept of mind control, emphasizing the power of the subconscious mind to influence thoughts, behaviors, and outcomes. Through a series of practical exercises and guided meditations, readers learn how to access deeper levels of consciousness, tap into their innate intuition, and reprogram limiting beliefs that may be hindering their progress.

Key themes addressed in the book include:

The Power of Visualization: Readers are introduced to the transformative practice of visualization, wherein they learn to mentally rehearse desired outcomes and manifest their goals with greater clarity and focus.

Mental Screening and Dream Control: The Silva Method teaches techniques for creating and manipulating mental images, allowing individuals to overcome obstacles, alleviate fears, and cultivate a more positive mindset.

Self-Reflection and Awareness: Through exercises in self-reflection and introspection, readers gain insight into their subconscious thought patterns, emotional responses, and behavioral tendencies, enabling them to cultivate greater self-awareness and emotional intelligence.

Practical Applications: The book explores real-world applications of mind control techniques, ranging from improving academic performance and enhancing creativity to overcoming phobias and achieving peak performance in various domains of life.

Holistic Well-Being: In addition to addressing mental and emotional well-being, the Silva Method emphasizes the interconnectedness of mind, body, and spirit. Readers are encouraged to adopt holistic practices that promote balance, vitality, and overall health.

Overall, "The Silva Mind Control Method" offers a comprehensive guide to unlocking the full potential of the human mind and harnessing its power to create positive change. Whether seeking personal growth, professional success, or spiritual fulfillment, readers will find valuable insights and practical tools to support their journey toward a more empowered and fulfilling life.

Your Transformative Journey

Embark on a transformative journey with the purposefully left blank pages beneath the Self-Reflection Questions and Final Evaluation Questions. These pages serve as your exclusive canvas for introspection as you navigate this meticulously crafted workbook. Take advantage of this opportunity to articulate your goals, intentions, and aspirations, transforming these blank spaces into a personal repository of your evolving self.

Delve into the recesses of your past experiences, capturing the nuances of thoughts and emotions that have molded the tapestry of your life. Through this process, you lay the foundation to assess your growth and progress as you approach the conclusion of this workbook.

This workbook is designed to facilitate a profound understanding of yourself, offering guidance to construct a roadmap for your healing journey within the expansive canvas of these blank pages. Your personal odyssey is uniquely yours, and there is no predefined right or wrong approach. Embrace vulnerability and engage in the process with an open mind. May this workbook be a cherished companion on your transformative path, guiding you toward self-discovery and growth.

Chapter 1 Summary: Using More of Your Mind in Special Ways

In the first chapter of "The Silva Mind Control Method," readers are introduced to the concept of tapping into higher intelligence through simple methods. The authors emphasize the idea of establishing a connection with a guiding wisdom that can empower individuals to overcome feelings of being out of touch or helpless. Through the Silva Method, readers are encouraged to explore and utilize their minds in unique ways to access this higher intelligence.

Notable Lessons

Establishing a direct connection with higher intelligence can bring about a sense of empowerment and guidance.

Simple techniques can be employed to access this higher intelligence, providing a lifelong resource for support and wisdom.

The Silva Method offers practical tools for individuals to tap into their innate potential and expand their mental capacities.

Feeling out of touch or helpless is not a permanent state; through practice and dedication, individuals can cultivate a strong connection with their inner wisdom.

There is a profound joy that accompanies the realization of being in tune with a higher intelligence that supports and guides individuals throughout their lives.

Self-Reflection Questions

How do you currently perceive your connection to higher intelligence or inner wisdom?

_____
_____
_____
_____
_____
_____
_____
_____
_____
_____
_____

What emotions arise when you consider the idea of feeling empowered and guided by a higher force?

_____
_____
_____
_____
_____
_____
_____
_____
_____
_____
_____

Have you ever experienced a moment of profound joy or clarity that felt connected to a deeper source of wisdom?

_____

_____

_____

_____

_____

_____

_____

_____

_____

_____

_____

In what areas of your life do you feel most out of touch or helpless, and how might tapping into higher intelligence help alleviate those feelings?

_____

_____

_____

_____

_____

_____

_____

_____

_____

_____

_____

_____

What simple techniques or practices have you tried in the past to access your inner wisdom, and what were the results?

_____

_____

_____

_____

_____

_____

_____

_____

_____

_____

Life Transforming Exercises

Take a few moments each day to quiet your mind through meditation or deep breathing exercises, allowing space for intuitive insights to arise.

Keep a journal to record any moments of clarity, inspiration, or guidance that come to you throughout the day.

Practice visualizing yourself connected to a vast source of wisdom and support, feeling the sense of empowerment and guidance it brings.

Engage in daily affirmations or positive self-talk to reinforce the belief in your ability to access higher intelligence.

Experiment with different techniques from the Silva Method presented in the chapter, such as mental imaging or creative visualization, and observe how they impact your sense of connection and empowerment.

Chapter 2 Summary: Meet José

Chapter 2 of "The Silva Mind Control Method" introduces readers to José Silva, the founder of the revolutionary program. Born into poverty in Laredo, Texas, José faced adversity from a young age after his father's death. Despite lacking formal education, José's determination led him to teach himself various skills, including radio repair through a correspondence course. His resourcefulness and commitment to learning set the stage for his later exploration into the realms of mind control and higher intelligence.

Notable Lessons

Adversity can be a catalyst for personal growth and development, propelling individuals to overcome obstacles and pursue their goals.

Self-education and lifelong learning are invaluable tools for empowerment and advancement, regardless of formal schooling.

Resourcefulness and determination are essential qualities for success, enabling individuals to find solutions even in challenging circumstances.

Opportunities for growth and improvement can arise unexpectedly, often in the midst of everyday experiences and interactions.

The journey from humble beginnings to significant achievements is marked by perseverance, resilience, and a willingness to seize opportunities for self-improvement.

Self-Reflection Questions

How do José Silva's early experiences with adversity and self-education resonate with your own life journey?

_____

_____

_____

_____

_____

_____

_____

_____

_____

_____

_____

Reflect on a time when you encountered unexpected opportunities for learning and growth. How did you respond, and what lessons did you take away from that experience?

_____

_____

_____

_____

_____

_____

_____

_____

_____

_____

_____

Consider the role of resourcefulness and determination in your pursuit of personal and professional goals. How have these qualities influenced your path to success?

_____

_____

_____

_____

_____

_____

_____

_____

_____

_____

_____

In what ways have you embraced self-education and lifelong learning outside of formal academic settings?

_____

_____

_____

_____

_____

_____

_____

_____

_____

_____

_____

_____

Reflect on the significance of perseverance and resilience in overcoming obstacles and achieving your aspirations, drawing inspiration from José Silva's story.

_____

_____

_____

_____

_____

_____

_____

_____

_____

_____

_____

Life Transforming Exercises

Take inventory of your current skills and knowledge, identifying areas where self-education and further learning could enhance your personal and professional development.

Explore new hobbies or interests that align with your passions and goals, committing to self-directed study and practice.

Set aside time each day for reading, listening to podcasts, or engaging in online courses to expand your understanding and expertise in areas of interest.

Reflect on past challenges or setbacks you've overcome, recognizing the resilience and determination that propelled you forward, and apply those lessons to current goals.

Practice gratitude for the opportunities and resources available to you on your journey of self-improvement, acknowledging the role of both adversity and growth in shaping your path.

Chapter 3 Summary: How to Meditate

Chapter 3 of "The Silva Mind Control Method" introduces readers to the fundamental practice of meditation as taught by José Silva. Meditation is presented as a tool for accessing the Alpha level of mind, where individuals can tap into their imagination and begin to solve problems. Through simple instructions, readers are guided to reach the meditative state, which is described as a crucial first step in the Silva Mind Control program for unlocking the body's healing powers and releasing tension.

Notable Lessons

Meditation is a foundational practice in the Silva Mind Control Method, providing access to the Alpha level of mind where problem-solving abilities are enhanced.

The act of meditation can help neutralize the activities of the mind that contribute to stress and illness, thereby promoting physical and mental well-being.

The body possesses innate healing mechanisms that are hindered by untrained minds; meditation serves to unleash these healing powers and restore energy wasted on tension.

Simple techniques, such as counting backward with closed eyes at a specific angle, can induce the Alpha brainwave state associated with relaxation and heightened mental clarity.

Reactions to meditation experiences vary among individuals, but consistent practice can deepen familiarity with the meditative state and its benefits over time.

Self-Reflection Questions

How do you currently incorporate meditation or relaxation practices into your daily routine, if at all?

_____

_____

_____

_____

_____

_____

_____

_____

_____

_____

_____

Reflect on any past experiences with meditation or similar practices. What sensations or thoughts did you encounter during those sessions?

_____

_____

_____

_____

_____

_____

_____

_____

_____

_____

_____

Consider the concept of the Alpha level of mind introduced in the chapter. How might accessing this state enhance your problem-solving abilities and creativity?

_____

_____

_____

_____

_____

_____

_____

_____

_____

_____

Explore any initial resistance or skepticism you may have towards meditation. What beliefs or assumptions influence your perception of its effectiveness?

_____

_____

_____

_____

_____

_____

_____

_____

_____

_____

Imagine integrating meditation into your daily life. How might cultivating a regular meditation practice impact your overall well-being and productivity?

_____

_____

_____

_____

_____

_____

_____

_____

_____

_____

Life Transforming Exercises

Dedicate 10-15 minutes each morning to the meditation technique described in the chapter, gradually increasing the duration as you become more comfortable with the practice.

Experiment with different eye positions and breathing techniques during meditation to discover what induces a deeper state of relaxation for you.

Keep a journal to track your experiences and observations before and after meditation sessions, noting any changes in mood, energy levels, or mental clarity.

Explore guided meditation recordings or apps to deepen your understanding of meditation practices and incorporate variety into your routine.

Share your meditation journey with a friend or family member, discussing your motivations, challenges, and insights gained from the practice.

Chapter 4 Summary: Dynamic Meditation

Chapter 4 of "The Silva Mind Control Method" introduces dynamic meditation as an alternative approach to passive meditation. José Silva discusses various methods, including focusing on sounds, breath, energy points, or external stimuli like music and dance, to reach a meditative state. Emphasizing the mind's capacity for organized, dynamic activities, José highlights the effectiveness of dynamic meditation in problem-solving. Readers are encouraged to move beyond passive techniques and utilize visualization to solve problems actively during meditation.

Notable Lessons

Dynamic meditation offers alternative approaches to passive meditation, utilizing various stimuli such as sounds, breath, and external sensations to reach a meditative state.

By engaging in dynamic meditation, individuals can tap into the mind's capacity for organized, dynamic activities, enhancing problem-solving abilities.

Visualization plays a crucial role in dynamic meditation, serving as a tool for actively solving problems and manifesting desired outcomes.

The ability to focus on pleasant memories or experiences before entering a meditative state can enhance relaxation and mental clarity.

Dynamic meditation provides a platform for exploring creativity, intuition, and problem-solving skills, fostering personal growth and development.

Self-Reflection Questions

How does the concept of dynamic meditation resonate with your current understanding of meditation practices?

_____

_____

_____

_____

_____

_____

_____

_____

_____

_____

Reflect on past experiences with different meditation techniques mentioned in the chapter (e.g., focusing on sounds, breath, or external stimuli). Which approach resonates most with you, and why?

_____

_____

_____

_____

_____

_____

_____

_____

_____

_____

_____

Consider the role of visualization in problem-solving during meditation. How do you typically approach problem-solving, and how might visualization enhance this process?

_____
_____
_____
_____
_____
_____
_____
_____
_____
_____

Think of a recent pleasant experience and reflect on its impact on your mood and mental state. How might recalling positive memories before meditation influence your practice?

_____
_____
_____
_____
_____
_____
_____
_____
_____
_____

Explore your beliefs and attitudes towards creativity and intuition. How might dynamic meditation serve as a vehicle for cultivating these qualities in your life?

_____

_____

_____

_____

_____

_____

_____

_____

_____

_____

_____

Life Transforming Exercises

Experiment with different dynamic meditation techniques mentioned in the chapter, such as focusing on sounds, breath, or external stimuli, to discover which method resonates most with you.

Before each dynamic meditation session, take a few moments to reflect on a recent pleasant experience or memory, allowing it to guide your mental state during the practice.

Incorporate visualization into your dynamic meditation sessions by actively solving problems or manifesting desired outcomes in your mind's eye.

Explore creative activities outside of meditation, such as drawing, writing, or dancing, to further enhance your problem-solving abilities and intuition.

Keep a journal to record insights, breakthroughs, and reflections from your dynamic meditation practice, tracking your progress and growth over time.

Chapter 5 Summary: Improving Memory

In Chapter 5 of "The Silva Mind Control Method," José Silva delves into memory improvement techniques. While these techniques can impress others and streamline daily tasks like recalling phone numbers, José emphasizes the importance of desire in effectively applying Mind Control methods. He suggests that using these techniques for trivial matters may lack the necessary motivation for success. José encourages readers to focus their efforts on significant tasks to harness the power of desire, belief, and expectancy in achieving memory enhancement.

Notable Lessons

Enhancing memory skills not only enhances one's ability to impress others and efficiently manage daily activities but also hinges significantly on personal motivation, belief, and expectancy.

When it comes to trivial matters, applying memory enhancement techniques might yield subpar results if one lacks the necessary drive and dedication.

The level of desire a person has plays a pivotal role in the success of their memory improvement endeavors, guiding them to prioritize tasks and allocate their efforts wisely.

Moreover, having unwavering belief in the efficacy of memory enhancement techniques is vital for optimizing their impact and attaining desired results.

Self-Reflection Questions

Reflect on your current approach to memory improvement. Do you prioritize important tasks or focus on trivial matters? How might your level of desire influence your success?

_____

_____

_____

_____

_____

_____

_____

_____

_____

_____

Consider instances where you've applied memory improvement techniques. Did your belief in their effectiveness impact the outcome? Why or why not?

_____

_____

_____

_____

_____

_____

_____

_____

_____

_____

_____

Explore the relationship between desire, belief, and expectancy in achieving goals. How can you cultivate a mindset that enhances memory enhancement efforts?

_____
_____
_____
_____
_____
_____
_____
_____
_____
_____

Think of a recent experience where memory played a significant role in achieving a goal or completing a task. How did your level of motivation and commitment influence your success?

_____
_____
_____
_____
_____
_____
_____
_____
_____
_____
_____

Reflect on the importance of prioritizing tasks and allocating resources effectively in memory enhancement. What strategies can you implement to ensure your efforts are focused on meaningful objectives?

_____

_____

_____

_____

_____

_____

_____

_____

_____

_____

_____

Life Transforming Exercises

Identify three significant tasks or goals that would benefit from improved memory skills, and commit to applying memory enhancement techniques to these areas.

Reflect on your beliefs about memory improvement. Challenge any limiting beliefs and affirm your confidence in your ability to enhance your memory effectively.

Create a visualization exercise where you imagine successfully recalling important information with ease and confidence. Practice this visualization regularly to reinforce belief and expectancy.

Prioritize tasks based on their significance and impact, allocating time and resources accordingly to maximize memory enhancement efforts.

Keep a journal to track your progress in memory improvement, recording successes, challenges, and insights gained from applying Mind Control techniques to important tasks.

Chapter 6 Summary: Speed Learning

Chapter 6 of "The Silva Mind Control Method" introduces Speed Learning as the next step in the program. José Silva outlines the progression from entering the meditative level to utilizing techniques like the Three Fingers Technique for instant recall. Speed Learning enhances concentration, improves information retention, and deepens understanding by combining learning at both the Beta and Alpha levels. José provides practical tips for implementing Speed Learning, emphasizing its effectiveness in various fields such as sales, academia, law, and entertainment.

Notable Lessons

Speed Learning involves utilizing techniques like the Three Fingers Technique to enhance concentration, improve information retention, and deepen understanding.

Mastery of the Three Fingers Technique enables instant access to the meditative level, facilitating active learning and recall during lectures or reading.

By incorporating learning at both the Beta and Alpha levels, Speed Learning accelerates the acquisition of knowledge while reinforcing memory recall.

Speed Learning techniques have proven valuable across diverse fields, including sales, academia, law, and entertainment, by enabling individuals to study less and learn more efficiently.

Practicing Speed Learning enhances confidence, effectiveness, and adaptability in various professional and academic pursuits.

Self-Reflection Questions

Reflect on your current study habits or learning techniques. How might incorporating Speed Learning principles enhance your ability to absorb and retain information?

_____

_____

_____

_____

_____

_____

_____

_____

_____

_____

Consider instances where you've struggled to concentrate during lectures or while studying. How could techniques like the Three Fingers Technique improve your focus and comprehension?

_____

_____

_____

_____

_____

_____

_____

_____

_____

_____

_____

Explore your beliefs about the relationship between study time and learning outcomes. How might adopting Speed Learning techniques challenge or reinforce these beliefs?

_____

_____

_____

_____

_____

_____

_____

_____

_____

_____

_____

Reflect on the potential applications of Speed Learning in your personal or professional life. In what areas could you benefit most from accelerated learning and improved memory recall?

_____

_____

_____

_____

_____

_____

_____

_____

_____

_____

_____

Imagine implementing Speed Learning techniques in your daily routine. How might this approach streamline your study habits, allowing you to achieve your academic or professional goals more efficiently?

_____

_____

_____

_____

_____

_____

_____

_____

_____

_____

Life Transforming Exercises

Practice the Three Fingers Technique daily to strengthen your ability to enter the meditative level quickly and effortlessly.

Experiment with recording lectures or key study materials and listening to them in the Alpha state using Speed Learning techniques for enhanced comprehension and retention.

Apply Speed Learning principles to a specific area of study or professional development, setting measurable goals for improvement in comprehension, recall, and efficiency.

Collaborate with peers or colleagues to exchange recorded materials and provide feedback on each other's Speed Learning techniques.

Keep a journal to track your progress in implementing Speed Learning techniques, noting any improvements in concentration, memory recall, and overall learning outcomes over time.

Chapter 7 Summary: Creative Sleep

In Chapter 7 of "The Silva Mind Control Method," José Silva introduces the concept of Creative Sleep, emphasizing the significance of dreams in problem-solving and personal development. Unlike Freudian dream analysis, Mind Control focuses on deliberately programming dreams to address specific issues. José shares personal experiences and anecdotes to illustrate the power of dream control, including his own lottery-winning dream. Through a three-step process, readers learn to enhance dream recall, program dreams to solve problems, and interpret dream symbolism for guidance and insight.

Notable Lessons

Dreams play a crucial role in problem-solving and personal insight, offering a window into the subconscious mind's wisdom and creativity.

Mind Control advocates deliberate dream programming to address specific challenges, leading to practical solutions and profound insights.

Dream recall can be enhanced through meditation and intention-setting before sleep, allowing individuals to access and interpret valuable dream content.

Dream interpretation in Mind Control differs from traditional Freudian analysis, focusing on the intentional creation and interpretation of dreams for practical guidance.

Dreams can serve as powerful tools for communication with Higher Intelligence, offering guidance and solutions in times of need or uncertainty.

Self-Reflection Questions

Reflect on a memorable dream you've had in the past. How might the content or symbolism of that dream relate to challenges or questions you were facing in your waking life?

_____

_____

_____

_____

_____

_____

_____

_____

_____

_____

Consider José Silva's lottery-winning dream and subsequent experiences. Do you believe his success was merely coincidence, or do you see it as evidence of a deeper connection to Higher Intelligence? Why?

_____

_____

_____

_____

_____

_____

_____

_____

Explore your beliefs about the purpose and significance of dreams in your life. How might intentional dream programming enhance your problem-solving abilities and personal growth?

_____
_____
_____
_____
_____
_____
_____
_____
_____
_____

Imagine implementing the three-step Dream Control technique in your own life. What specific challenges or questions would you address through intentional dream programming, and what outcomes do you hope to achieve?

_____
_____
_____
_____
_____
_____
_____
_____
_____

Reflect on the concept of "programmed hunches" mentioned by José Silva. How might trusting your intuition and subconscious insights, developed through Dream Control practice, influence your decision-making and problem-solving abilities?

_____

_____

_____

_____

_____

_____

_____

_____

_____

_____

Life Transforming Exercises

Before going to sleep each night, practice meditation and affirmations to program your subconscious mind for dream recall and problem-solving.

Keep a dream journal by your bedside and record any dreams or fragments of dreams upon waking, focusing on symbols, emotions, and recurring themes.

Experiment with programming specific dreams to address current challenges or questions, using affirmations and visualization techniques during pre-sleep meditation.

Practice interpreting dream symbolism and extracting insights or solutions from your dreams, trusting your intuition and subconscious guidance.

Explore the connection between your dreams and waking life experiences, looking for patterns or correlations that may provide deeper understanding and guidance.

Chapter 8 Summary: Your Words Have Power

Chapter 8 emphasizes the profound impact of words on shaping our reality and influencing our health. It explores how the language we use can either empower or hinder us, affecting not only our mental state but also our physical well-being. Through various examples and anecdotes, the chapter highlights the transformative power of positive affirmations and mindful language in fostering health and resilience.

Notable Lessons

Words have the power to shape our reality and influence our health, as they can evoke physiological responses in our bodies.

Negative language can create a cycle of negativity, affecting both mental outlook and physical health over time.

Positive affirmations, when repeated with conviction and consistency, can initiate profound changes in attitude and well-being.

The mind-body connection is strong, with our thoughts and words capable of triggering physiological responses and affecting our overall health.

Simple affirmations, such as those advocated by Dr. Émile Coué, can have significant therapeutic effects, demonstrating the potency of self-directed healing.

Self-Reflection Questions

How aware are you of the language you use in your daily life, and do you believe it has an impact on your well-being?

_____

_____

_____

_____

_____

_____

_____

_____

_____

_____

Reflect on a time when positive or negative language significantly influenced your mood or physical state.

_____

_____

_____

_____

_____

_____

_____

_____

_____

_____

_____

How do you currently incorporate affirmations or positive self-talk into your routine, and what changes do you observe when practicing them consistently?

_____
_____
_____
_____
_____
_____
_____
_____
_____
_____
_____

Consider the story of the soldier who overcame health challenges through positive affirmations. How might his experience inspire changes in your own approach to health and self-care?

_____
_____
_____
_____
_____
_____
_____
_____
_____
_____
_____

Reflect on the concept of the mind-body connection and its implications for your overall health and resilience. How might you leverage this connection to promote healing and well-being in your life?

_____

_____

_____

_____

_____

_____

_____

_____

_____

_____

_____

Life Transforming Exercises

Begin each day with a series of positive affirmations tailored to your goals and well-being, repeating them with sincerity and belief.

Keep a journal to track the language you use throughout the day, noting any patterns of negativity and identifying opportunities for positive reframing.

Practice mindfulness meditation to cultivate awareness of your thoughts and language, learning to observe them without judgment and redirecting negative self-talk.

Experiment with Dr. Coué's method of autosuggestion by repeating affirmations such as "Every day, in every way, I am getting better and better" to initiate self-healing processes.

Engage in daily self-care rituals that prioritize positive self-talk and affirmations, recognizing the profound impact of language on your overall health and well-being.

Chapter 9 Summary: The Power of Imagination

Chapter 9 delves into the significance of imagination and its transformative potential in achieving personal goals and overcoming obstacles. It explores how willpower, often perceived as brute force, can be complemented and strengthened by harnessing the creative power of the mind. Through anecdotes and insights, the chapter illuminates the ways in which imagination can be cultivated and utilized to enhance motivation, problem-solving, and goal attainment.

Notable Lessons

Imagination serves as a potent tool in bolstering willpower, offering a creative approach to surmounting obstacles and achieving desired outcomes.

Rather than relying solely on sheer determination, individuals can tap into their imaginative faculties to envision solutions, visualize success, and maintain motivation.

Cultivating a rich inner world through imagination enables individuals to explore possibilities, devise innovative strategies, and adapt flexibly to challenges.

The power of imagination lies not only in envisioning future goals but also in shaping present actions and attitudes, fostering resilience and resourcefulness.

By integrating imagination into goal-setting and problem-solving processes, individuals can cultivate a sense of agency and empowerment, unlocking new potentials for growth and achievement.

Self-Reflection Questions

Recall a moment when creativity proved instrumental in surmounting a challenge or reaching a milestone. How did your imaginative approach diverge from traditional problem-solving methods?

_____

_____

_____

_____

_____

_____

_____

_____

_____

_____

Reflect on the interplay between determination and imagination in your personal journey. How could harnessing your creative faculties bolster your drive and concentration towards your objectives?

_____

_____

_____

_____

_____

_____

_____

_____

_____

_____

Examine the facets of your daily routine where imagination comes into play. Can you identify areas where leveraging your inventive abilities could better address hurdles or pursue ambitions?

_____

_____

_____

_____

_____

_____

_____

_____

_____

_____

Contemplate the significance of visualization in accomplishing goals. How might vividly picturing success and outlining the necessary steps impact your actions and achievements?

_____

_____

_____

_____

_____

_____

_____

_____

_____

_____

_____

Ponder the notion of "mental practice" and its utility in preparing for forthcoming trials or endeavors. How might engaging in imaginative rehearsal bolster your assurance and performance across various domains?

_____

_____

_____

_____

_____

_____

_____

_____

_____

_____

_____

Life Transforming Exercises

Set aside dedicated time each day for imaginative exploration, engaging in activities such as creative writing, visual art, or guided visualization exercises.

Practice visualizing your goals and aspirations with vivid detail, imagining yourself succeeding and experiencing the emotions associated with achievement.

Experiment with "future self" visualization exercises, envisioning your ideal self in specific areas of life and identifying actionable steps to move closer to that vision.

Use imaginative problem-solving techniques, such as brainstorming or role-playing, to explore multiple perspectives and generate innovative solutions to challenges.

Incorporate visualization and imagination into your daily goal-setting routine, reinforcing your commitment to personal growth and development through creative visualization techniques.

Chapter 10 Summary: Using Your Mind to Improve Your Health

Chapter 10 delves into the profound connection between the mind and the body, highlighting the remarkable potential of the Silva Mind Control Method in fostering self-healing. The author shares numerous anecdotes of individuals who have experienced significant improvements in their health through Mind Control techniques, underscoring the inherent power of the mind in influencing physical well-being. Despite ongoing research into the mind-body relationship, the efficacy of psychic healing methods like Mind Control remains evident, offering a holistic approach to health that is free from harmful side effects associated with conventional medicine.

Notable Lessons

The mind wields remarkable influence over the body's capacity to heal, evident in the multitude of self-healing accounts documented by practitioners of Mind Control.

Utilizing psychic healing modalities akin to those found in Mind Control offers a gentle and efficacious alternative to conventional medical interventions, free from adverse effects.

While Mind Control doesn't promise flawless health, its methodologies can significantly fortify the body's innate healing mechanisms, augmenting its resilience against illness.

Engaging in Mind Control practices facilitates the mitigation of detrimental thoughts and emotions, empowering the body to operate optimally and engage in self-restoration.

Integral to Mind Control techniques is mental visualization, empowering individuals to direct their healing energies toward specific areas of concern within the body.

Self-Reflection Questions

Reflect on your own perceptions of psychic healing and its efficacy compared to conventional medicine. How do these perceptions influence your approach to managing your health?

_____

_____

_____

_____

_____

_____

_____

_____

_____

_____

Consider instances where you have experienced the mind-body connection in your own life. How have your thoughts and emotions impacted your physical well-being?

_____

_____

_____

_____

_____

_____

_____

_____

_____

_____

_____

Explore any hesitations or skepticism you may have about utilizing Mind Control techniques for self-healing. What factors contribute to these doubts, and how might you overcome them?

_____

_____

_____

_____

_____

_____

_____

_____

_____

_____

Imagine the ideal state of health and well-being for yourself. How can practicing Mind Control techniques help you move closer to realizing this vision?

_____

_____

_____

_____

_____

_____

_____

_____

_____

_____

_____

Reflect on the role of visualization in the healing process. How might mentally experiencing an illness or ailment aid in directing your body's healing energies to the affected areas?

_____

_____

_____

_____

_____

_____

_____

_____

_____

_____

Life Transforming Exercises

Dedicate regular time to practicing Mind Control techniques, focusing on positive affirmations and mental imagery aimed at promoting self-healing.

Create a personalized mental script outlining your desire for optimal health and well-being, incorporating positive language and intentions.

Utilize the mental screen visualization technique to envision the state of wellness you aspire to achieve, reinforcing your body's innate capacity for healing.

Cultivate a loving and forgiving mindset through mindfulness practices, fostering a harmonious environment for self-repair to occur.

Journal about your experiences with Mind Control techniques, noting any changes in your physical health and emotional well-being over time.

Chapter 11 Summary: An Intimate Exercise for Lovers

In Chapter 11, the authors explore the concept of creating deep intimacy between partners using techniques from the Silva Mind Control Method. They discuss the importance of good marriages for overall well-being and introduce an exercise designed to enhance intimacy through meditation and shared experience. This exercise aims to deepen the connection between partners and strengthen their bond on both a physical and psychic level.

Notable Lessons

Deep and prolonged meditation can foster connections between minds, leading to a profound sense of intimacy.

Intentional creation of intimate experiences can strengthen the bond between partners, surpassing even the connections formed in group settings like the Mind Control course.

Physical closeness between partners can positively influence their energy fields, enhancing compatibility and connection.

Sexuality is viewed as a spectrum of experiences, beyond mere technique, emphasizing the importance of deep, meditative engagement for a fulfilling intimate life.

Becoming psychically sensitive can enhance marital understanding and satisfaction, offering a pathway to deeper connection and harmony.

Self-Reflection Questions

How does the concept of shared experiences in deep meditation resonate with your understanding of intimacy?

_____

_____

_____

_____

_____

_____

_____

_____

_____

_____

Reflect on a place or memory that holds significant meaning for you and your partner. How might revisiting this memory deepen your connection?

_____

_____

_____

_____

_____

_____

_____

_____

_____

_____

_____

Consider the spectrum of experiences within sexuality mentioned in the chapter. How do you currently approach intimacy with your partner, and what changes, if any, would you like to make?

_____

_____

_____

_____

_____

_____

_____

_____

_____

_____

Explore your thoughts on psychic sensitivity and its role in enhancing marital understanding. How open are you to exploring this aspect of connection with your partner?

_____

_____

_____

_____

_____

_____

_____

_____

_____

_____

_____

Reflect on the cautionary note regarding the misuse of intimate experiences. How can you ensure mutual understanding and agreement when engaging in practices aimed at deepening your connection with your partner?

_____

_____

_____

_____

_____

_____

_____

_____

_____

_____

_____

Life Transforming Exercises

Choose a place of shared happiness or create a new one with your partner. Practice deep meditation together, focusing on mutual relaxation and connection.

Engage in a guided meditation where you and your partner describe the surroundings of your chosen place, fostering a shared sensory experience.

Express your commitment to each other's happiness during the meditation, emphasizing mutual care and support.

Experiment with prolonged eye contact during silent communion, allowing for a deeper level of connection.

Reflect on the quality of your physical closeness and its impact on your relationship. Consider practical steps to enhance physical proximity and deepen energetic compatibility with your partner.

Chapter 12 Summary: You Can Practice Esp

Chapter 12 delves into the reality of extrasensory perception (ESP) and its application within the framework of the Silva Mind Control Method. The authors challenge the traditional understanding of ESP terminology and introduce the concept of Effective Sensory Projection (ESP), emphasizing an active role in accessing information beyond the five senses. Through practical exercises, Mind Control students explore the potential of ESP to perceive and interact with distant or inaccessible environments.

Notable Lessons

ESP, or Effective Sensory Projection, is a tangible phenomenon supported by empirical evidence, allowing individuals to access information beyond the five senses.

The terminology of "extrasensory perception" may limit our understanding of ESP, as it implies passivity. Instead, the concept of Effective Sensory Projection highlights the active role individuals play in accessing non-local information.

Mind Control techniques involve more than mere perception; practitioners actively project their awareness to access desired information.

Practical exercises, such as those described in the chapter, offer a hands-on approach to developing ESP abilities, allowing individuals to interact with distant environments and objects.

ESP expands the boundaries of human perception, enabling individuals to transcend limitations of time, space, and sensory apparatus.

Self-Reflection Questions

How does the concept of Effective Sensory Projection challenge your understanding of traditional ESP?

_____

_____

_____

_____

_____

_____

_____

_____

_____

_____

Reflect on your beliefs regarding the existence of non-local information and its accessibility beyond the five senses.

_____

_____

_____

_____

_____

_____

_____

_____

_____

_____

Consider the implications of actively projecting awareness versus passively perceiving information. How might this shift in perspective influence your approach to ESP development?

_____

_____

_____

_____

_____

_____

_____

_____

_____

_____

_____

Explore your experiences with intuition or gut feelings. How do these experiences align with the concept of ESP as described in the chapter?

_____

_____

_____

_____

_____

_____

_____

_____

_____

_____

_____

Imagine engaging in the practical exercises outlined in the chapter. What emotions or thoughts arise as you contemplate interacting with distant environments or objects through ESP?

_____

_____

_____

_____

_____

_____

_____

_____

_____

_____

_____

_____

Life Transforming Exercises

Practice imagining yourself in a familiar place and explore it mentally.

Try focusing on something far away and notice any feelings or sensations that come up.

Imagine being in a different place and pay attention to what it's like there - what you see, hear, smell, and feel.

Think about how accessing non-local information could help you make decisions or solve problems in your daily life.

Keep a journal to track any intuitive experiences you have and how they affect your progress in developing ESP abilities.

Chapter 13 Summary: Form Your Own Practice Group

Chapter 13 encourages readers to form their own practice groups to further develop their mental abilities, particularly in the context of Effective Sensory Projection (ESP). The authors provide guidelines for conducting group sessions, emphasizing patience, cooperation, and the importance of controlled conditions. Through anecdotes and practical advice, they demonstrate the potential for growth and success in psychic development, highlighting the journey of perseverance and self-discovery.

Notable Lessons

Developing psychic abilities, such as ESP, requires steady and prolonged practice, preferably within a supportive group setting.

Group exercises, conducted under controlled conditions, facilitate the exploration and refinement of psychic skills, such as Effective Sensory Projection.

Success in psychic development may vary among individuals, and early setbacks do not necessarily indicate a lack of ability.

Patience, cooperation, and a willingness to learn from both successes and failures are essential for progress in psychic development.

Personal experiences and anecdotes illustrate the diverse pathways to success in psychic development and the importance of perseverance in the journey.

Self-Reflection Questions

Reflect on your understanding of psychic development and the potential benefits of forming a practice group. How might collaborating with others enhance your journey?

_____

_____

_____

_____

_____

_____

_____

_____

_____

_____

_____

Consider the guidelines provided for conducting group sessions. How do these principles align with your beliefs about effective learning and development?

_____

_____

_____

_____

_____

_____

_____

_____

_____

_____

_____

_____

Explore your thoughts on success and setbacks in psychic development. How do you respond to challenges, and what strategies might you employ to maintain motivation and perseverance?

_____

_____

_____

_____

_____

_____

_____

_____

_____

_____

Reflect on the anecdote of Jim Needham's journey in psychic development. What lessons can be drawn from his perseverance and eventual success?

_____

_____

_____

_____

_____

_____

_____

_____

_____

_____

_____

Imagine yourself participating in a psychic practice group. What expectations do you have, and how do you envision contributing to the group's collective growth and learning?

_____

_____

_____

_____

_____

_____

_____

_____

_____

_____

_____

Life Transforming Exercises

Organize or join a psychic practice group with like-minded individuals, following the guidelines outlined in the chapter for conducting group sessions.

Practice Effective Sensory Projection exercises within the group, focusing on exploring and interacting with distant environments or objects.

Engage in case work exercises, pairing off as practiced in Mind Control classes, and take turns acting as both the psychic and the orientologist.

Reflect on your experiences and observations during group sessions, noting any insights or challenges encountered, and discuss them with fellow group members.

Maintain patience and perseverance in your psychic development journey, recognizing that success may come with time and dedicated practice.

Chapter 14 Summary: How to Help Others With Mind Control

Chapter 14 delves into the practice of psychic healing within the framework of the Silva Mind Control Method. The authors emphasize the power of intention and visualization in directing mental energy towards healing. Through anecdotes and practical guidance, they illustrate the effectiveness of psychic healing techniques and dispel common misconceptions about the process.

Notable Lessons

Psychic healing involves harnessing mental energy through focused intention and visualization to promote healing in others.

The power of visualization is central to psychic healing, as practitioners project images of health and vitality onto the mental screen.

Confidence and belief in the healing process are essential for successful outcomes, as the mind's receptivity to positive suggestions influences the effectiveness of psychic healing.

Psychic healing can be practiced remotely, without the need for physical proximity to the recipient, and is governed by universal laws of intention and belief.

The practice of psychic healing is not physically draining for the healer; instead, it often results in a sense of upliftment and well-being.

Self-Reflection Question

Reflect on your understanding of psychic healing and its potential impact on promoting wellness in others. How do your beliefs align with the principles outlined in the chapter?

_____

_____

_____

_____

_____

_____

_____

_____

_____

_____

Consider the role of intention and visualization in psychic healing. How might you cultivate confidence in your ability to direct mental energy towards healing outcomes?

_____

_____

_____

_____

_____

_____

_____

_____

_____

_____

_____

Explore any preconceived notions or doubts you may have about the effectiveness of remote healing practices. How open are you to exploring alternative methods of promoting health and well-being?

_____

_____

_____

_____

_____

_____

_____

_____

_____

_____

_____

Reflect on the anecdote of José Silva's healing experience with the parish priest. What insights can be drawn from his approach to healing and the power of visualization?

_____

_____

_____

_____

_____

_____

_____

_____

_____

_____

_____

Contemplate the significance of secrecy in psychic healing practices, as discussed in the chapter. How might keeping healing intentions private enhance their effectiveness, and what implications does this have for your own practice?

_____

_____

_____

_____

_____

_____

_____

_____

_____

_____

_____

Life Transforming Exercises

Practice visualizing individuals in perfect health on your mental screen, focusing on projecting images of vitality and well-being.

Experiment with remote healing techniques by directing positive intentions towards individuals in need of healing, regardless of physical proximity.

Cultivate confidence in your ability to promote healing through mental projection, reinforcing your belief in the effectiveness of psychic healing.

Explore the concept of secrecy in healing practices by keeping your healing work private and observing any changes in its effectiveness.

Reflect on your experiences with psychic healing exercises, noting any shifts in belief, perception, or well-being, and document your observations for future reference.

Chapter 15 Summary: Some Speculations

Chapter 15 of "The Silva Mind Control Method" explores the author's reflections and speculations on various aspects of human consciousness, the universe, and spirituality. Drawing from personal experiences, scientific principles, and philosophical inquiries, the chapter delves into topics such as the nature of reality, the perception of time, the existence of higher intelligence, and the evolution of human consciousness.

Notable Lessons

Science and spirituality need not conflict; the author's discoveries in mind control align with various religious beliefs and scientific principles.

The universe operates according to laws, and human consciousness can influence and interact with these laws through focused intention and energy.

Reality is subjective and influenced by individual perception, with energy being the fundamental essence of all existence.

Time is a multifaceted concept, perceived differently depending on one's state of consciousness, with the potential for precognition and manipulation through meditation.

Higher intelligence, distinct from the traditional concept of God, represents a continuum of consciousness accessible through focused communication and prayer.

Self-Reflection Questions

Reflect on the author's assertion that science and spirituality can coexist harmoniously. How does this perspective challenge or align with your own beliefs about the relationship between science and faith?

_____

_____

_____

_____

_____

_____

_____

_____

_____

_____

Consider the implications of the author's view of reality as a subjective construct shaped by individual perception. How might this perspective influence your understanding of personal experiences and interactions with the world?

_____

_____

_____

_____

_____

_____

_____

_____

_____

_____

Explore your thoughts on the nature of time, as discussed in the chapter. How do cultural, philosophical, and scientific perspectives shape your understanding of time as a concept?

Contemplate the distinction between higher intelligence and the traditional concept of God proposed by the author. How does this differentiation resonate with or challenge your beliefs about spirituality and divine existence?

Reflect on the author's speculation about the future evolution of human consciousness. How might the development of psychic abilities and expanded consciousness impact society and individual experiences?

Life Transforming Exercises

Engage in a meditation practice focused on exploring your perception of time, allowing yourself to move freely between past, present, and future states of consciousness.

Experiment with visualizing energy flow within your body and surroundings, observing how thoughts and intentions influence energetic patterns.

Practice prayer or focused communication with higher intelligence, seeking guidance or clarity on specific life decisions or challenges.

Reflect on your beliefs about the relationship between science, spirituality, and consciousness, considering how these beliefs shape your worldview and daily experiences.

Explore the potential for personal evolution and expanded consciousness through mindfulness practices, journaling, or engaging in discussions with like-minded individuals.

Chapter 16 Summary: A Checklist

Chapter 16 of "The Silva Mind Control Method" provides a comprehensive checklist of techniques outlined in previous chapters, aimed at aiding readers in mastering the various practices introduced throughout the book. By offering a condensed overview of key methods for meditation, problem-solving, visualization, recall enhancement, dream interpretation, habit control, psychic functioning, healing, and relationship improvement, the chapter serves as a convenient reference guide for readers to optimize their mind control practice.

Notable Lessons

Achieving mastery in mind control techniques demands ongoing practice and occasional review to sustain skillfulness.

Various techniques exist for boosting mental abilities, solving problems, remembering, interpreting dreams, managing habits, tapping into psychic abilities, promoting healing, and enhancing relationships.

Each technique serves a unique purpose and can be customized to suit individual preferences and requirements.

Consistent practice builds familiarity and proficiency with chosen techniques, enabling greater adaptability in tackling different life situations.

A structured approach to mind control supports personal development, self-betterment, and the achievement of desired goals across various life domains.

Self-Reflection Questions

Which mind control techniques do you find most appealing, and why? How do these methods align with your personal goals and ambitions?

_____

_____

_____

_____

_____

_____

_____

_____

_____

_____

Reflect on your current use of mind control techniques. Have you overlooked any practices? How might reintegrating them improve your well-being?

_____

_____

_____

_____

_____

_____

_____

_____

_____

_____

Consider the effectiveness of the techniques listed for addressing specific challenges in your life. Which ones do you expect to be most helpful, and why?

_____
_____
_____
_____
_____
_____
_____
_____
_____
_____
_____

Explore any difficulties you've faced in consistently applying mind control techniques. What strategies can you use to overcome these obstacles and maintain a regular routine?

_____
_____
_____
_____
_____
_____
_____
_____
_____
_____
_____

Think about how mastering mind control techniques could impact your life, relationships, and growth. How do you plan to incorporate them into your daily life for lasting development and happiness?

_____

_____

_____

_____

_____

_____

_____

_____

_____

_____

_____

Life Transforming Exercises

Create a personalized mind control practice schedule, allocating dedicated time each day for meditation, visualization, problem-solving, and other techniques based on your priorities and objectives.

Experiment with incorporating different mind control techniques into your daily routine, observing how each method influences your mental clarity, emotional well-being, and productivity.

Keep a journal to track your progress and experiences with mind control techniques, noting any insights, challenges, or breakthroughs encountered along the way.

Engage in regular self-reflection sessions to assess your growth and development in utilizing mind control practices, identifying areas for improvement and refinement.

Establish accountability measures, such as setting goals or sharing progress with a supportive friend or mentor, to maintain consistency and motivation in your mind control journey.

Chapter 17 Summary: A Psychiatrist Works With Mind Control

Chapter 17 delves into the collaboration between José Silva's Mind Control method and psychiatry, highlighting Dr. Carl McKenzie's exploration of its potential benefits and risks. Dr. McKenzie's interest was piqued by observations of participants utilizing deep levels of consciousness in Mind Control classes, prompting him to conduct a study on psychiatric patients undergoing the training. Over four and a half years, 189 patients, including those with psychological vulnerabilities, volunteered for the study, revealing promising outcomes in terms of increased emotional energy and improved outlook for many participants.

Notable Lessons

Deep exploration of consciousness through Mind Control techniques offers potential benefits for individuals, including enhanced emotional well-being and increased energy levels.

Collaborative efforts between Mind Control practitioners and psychiatry can provide valuable insights into the therapeutic applications and effects of mind-control practices.

Careful observation and systematic studies are essential for understanding the impact of Mind Control techniques on individuals, particularly those with psychological vulnerabilities.

The integration of Mind Control into therapeutic settings requires cautious consideration of potential risks and benefits, emphasizing the importance of informed practice and ethical considerations.

Research initiatives that combine scientific rigor with experiential exploration can contribute to a deeper understanding of the mind-body connection and the potential for self-directed healing.

Self-Reflection Questions

Think about your experiences with mind control techniques or similar practices. How have they affected your emotional well-being and overall perspective on life?

_____

_____

_____

_____

_____

_____

_____

_____

_____

_____

Consider the ethical considerations of using mind control techniques in therapy, especially for people with psychological vulnerabilities. What measures would need to be in place to ensure safe and effective use?

_____

_____

_____

_____

_____

_____

_____

_____

_____

_____

_____

_____

Explore the potential risks and benefits of delving deeply into consciousness with mind control methods. How can practitioners minimize risks while maximizing the therapeutic benefits?

_____

_____

_____

_____

_____

_____

_____

_____

_____

_____

_____

Think about the potential for collaboration between mind control practitioners and psychiatric professionals to advance our understanding of consciousness and mental health. What challenges and opportunities might arise in such partnerships?

_____

_____

_____

_____

_____

_____

_____

_____

_____

_____

_____

Imagine how mind control could become a part of mainstream therapy in the future. How might these practices adapt to meet new mental health needs and promote overall well-being?

_____
_____
_____
_____
_____
_____
_____
_____
_____
_____
_____

Life Transforming Exercises

Engage in regular self-monitoring and reflection on the effects of Mind Control practices on your emotional state, energy levels, and overall well-being.

Explore collaborative opportunities with mental health professionals or support groups to share experiences and insights gained from Mind Control practices.

Conduct a literature review on the intersection of consciousness exploration and mental health, identifying key findings and areas for further research or personal exploration.

Practice ethical decision-making in the application of Mind Control techniques, considering the potential impact on yourself and others before engaging in deep consciousness exploration.

Foster a supportive and inclusive community of practitioners and researchers interested in the therapeutic applications of Mind

Control, promoting dialogue, collaboration, and responsible practice.

Chapter 18 Summary: Your Self-Esteem Will Soar

In Chapter 18, the transformative power of the Silva Mind Control Method on self-esteem is explored through various studies and testimonials. The chapter emphasizes breaking free from limiting beliefs to discover newfound freedoms and strengths. Through Mind Control, individuals, including students and those facing personal challenges like addiction or poverty, experience significant improvements in self-image and confidence. Scientific research, including studies conducted in educational settings, demonstrates the consistent positive impact of Mind Control on ego strength and self-assurance.

Notable Lessons

Investing time in exploring the capabilities of the mind can lead to the discovery of inner strengths and newfound freedoms.

Limiting beliefs about oneself can be shattered through the practice of Mind Control, leading to a significant boost in self-esteem.

Mind Control techniques promote greater self-direction and problem-solving abilities, fostering increased ego strength and resilience.

Scientific research validates the transformative effects of Mind Control on individuals from diverse backgrounds, including students, addicts, prisoners, and those in poverty.

Consistent practice of Mind Control can lead to lasting improvements in self-image and confidence, empowering individuals to navigate life's challenges with greater resilience.

Self-Reflection Questions

How do limiting beliefs about yourself impact your daily life and interactions with others? Reflect on specific instances where these beliefs may have influenced your behavior or decisions.

_____

_____

_____

_____

_____

_____

_____

_____

_____

_____

Consider a time when you achieved something you initially believed was beyond your capabilities. What factors contributed to your success, and how did it affect your self-esteem?

_____

_____

_____

_____

_____

_____

_____

_____

_____

_____

_____

Reflect on the concept of ego strength and its importance in navigating life's challenges. How do you currently cultivate and maintain your sense of self-assurance?

_____

_____

_____

_____

_____

_____

_____

_____

_____

Explore the role of mindset in shaping one's self-esteem. How might adopting a growth mindset, focused on learning and development, contribute to a more positive self-image?

_____

_____

_____

_____

_____

_____

_____

_____

_____

_____

Imagine your ideal level of self-esteem and confidence. What steps can you take, starting today, to move closer to that ideal state? How might Mind Control techniques support you in this journey?

_____

_____

_____

_____

_____

_____

_____

_____

_____

_____

_____

_____

Life Transforming Exercises

Practice affirmations every day to strengthen positive self-beliefs and combat negative thinking.

Use visualization exercises to picture yourself reaching your goals and conquering challenges with confidence.

Maintain a journal to monitor your development and reflect on moments of growth and success.

Find supportive communities or mentorship programs to connect with others on a similar path and gain encouragement.

Set clear, attainable goals for yourself and celebrate each step forward, acknowledging your achievements and potential for continued progress.

Chapter 19 Summary: Mind Control in the Business World

Chapter 19 explores the application of the Silva Mind Control Method in the business world, showcasing how individuals and companies have benefited from its techniques. Through various anecdotes and examples, the chapter illustrates how Mind Control has led to improved performance, problem-solving abilities, and overall success in professional endeavors. From salesmanship to entrepreneurship, the transformative impact of Mind Control is evident across diverse industries and roles.

Notable Lessons

Embracing the principles of Mind Control can lead to a shift in perspective, transforming challenges into opportunities for growth and success.

The cultivation of a positive attitude and belief in one's abilities is integral to achieving success in business and personal endeavors.

Mind Control techniques, such as visualization and positive affirmations, can enhance performance and effectiveness in various professional roles.

The application of Mind Control extends beyond individual success to collective achievements, fostering innovation and collaboration within teams and organizations.

Mind Control empowers individuals to tap into their innate creativity and intuition, leading to novel solutions and breakthroughs in problem-solving.

Self-Reflection Questions

How do you currently approach challenges and setbacks in your professional life? Consider how adopting a more positive mindset could influence your ability to overcome obstacles.

_____
_____
_____
_____
_____
_____
_____
_____
_____
_____
_____

Reflect on a time when you achieved success in your career. What role did belief in yourself and your abilities play in that accomplishment?

_____
_____
_____
_____
_____
_____
_____
_____
_____
_____
_____
_____

Explore the concept of intuition and its relevance in decision-making within the business world. How might cultivating your intuition enhance your effectiveness in problem-solving and innovation?

_____

_____

_____

_____

_____

_____

_____

_____

_____

Consider the importance of teamwork and collaboration in achieving business goals. How can Mind Control techniques support effective communication and synergy among team members?

_____

_____

_____

_____

_____

_____

_____

_____

_____

_____

_____

Imagine your ideal professional trajectory. How can you leverage Mind Control principles to manifest your career aspirations and drive success in your chosen field?

_____

_____

_____

_____

_____

_____

_____

_____

_____

_____

Life Transforming Exercises

Practice daily visualization exercises to envision yourself achieving your professional goals and overcoming obstacles with confidence and ease.

Develop a habit of positive self-talk and affirmations to reinforce belief in your capabilities and foster a resilient mindset.

Experiment with creative problem-solving techniques, such as brainstorming or mind mapping, to generate innovative solutions to business challenges.

Engage in regular meditation sessions to quiet the mind, enhance focus, and tap into your intuition for informed decision-making.

Cultivate a supportive network of like-minded individuals or mentors who can provide encouragement, guidance, and accountability on your professional journey.

Chapter 20 Summary: Where Do We Go From Here?

Chapter 20 explores the journey of self-discovery and continued growth after mastering the Silva Mind Control Method. It presents various paths for further development, emphasizing the importance of integrating and refining the techniques learned in the course. Through anecdotes and insights, the chapter delves into the profound transformations experienced by Mind Control graduates and the limitless potential of the human mind.

Notable Lessons

Continued exploration and practice of Mind Control techniques lead to deeper self-discovery and realization of the innate powers of the mind.

Specializing in one technique may yield initial results, but embracing the full spectrum of Mind Control exercises fosters comprehensive development and mastery.

Mind Control is a cohesive system of mental exercises that complement each other, enhancing overall effectiveness and results.

Achieving mastery in Mind Control involves converting problems into projects and manifesting desired outcomes with confidence and purpose.

The journey of self-discovery through Mind Control unveils a profound understanding of one's purpose and the interconnectedness of all life.

Self-Reflection Questions

Reflect on your current approach to personal growth and development. How might integrating Mind Control techniques enhance your journey of self-discovery?

_____

_____

_____

_____

_____

_____

_____

_____

_____

_____

_____

Consider the concept of mastering Mind Control versus specializing in a specific technique. Which approach resonates with you, and why?

_____

_____

_____

_____

_____

_____

_____

_____

_____

_____

Explore instances in your life where you've experienced the interconnectedness of events or sensed intuitive guidance. How does this align with the principles of Mind Control?

_____
_____
_____
_____
_____
_____
_____
_____
_____
_____

Imagine achieving a state of "firm certainty" about the purpose and potential of your life. What steps can you take to deepen your understanding and alignment with this vision?

_____
_____
_____
_____
_____
_____
_____
_____
_____
_____
_____

Reflect on the anecdotal experiences shared in the chapter. How do these stories inspire and inform your own exploration of Mind Control and self-discovery?

_____

_____

_____

_____

_____

_____

_____

_____

_____

_____

_____

Life Transforming Exercises

Regularly practice and refine various mind control techniques like Dream Control, Mental Screen visualization, and Effective Sensory Projection.

Adopt a mindset that turns problems into projects, seeing challenges as opportunities for growth and creative problem-solving.

Experiment with integrating mind control techniques into everyday situations like decision-making, problem-solving, and goal-setting to improve effectiveness and achieve desired outcomes.

Delve into your mind's depths through meditation and visualization exercises, seeking insights into your purpose and potential for growth.

Take charge of your own self-discovery journey, acting as the director of research, and tapping into your mind's power to explore new realms of consciousness and understanding.

Dear Esteemed Readers,

I want to express my sincerest congratulations and heartfelt gratitude to each and every one of you for journeying through the chapters of our workbook for "The Silva Mind Control Method" by José Silva and Philip Miele. Your dedication to personal growth and self-discovery is truly commendable, and I am deeply appreciative of the time and effort you have invested in exploring the transformative teachings within these pages.

Throughout this revolutionary program, you have delved into the depths of your own mind, unlocking new insights, and gaining valuable tools for personal empowerment. Your commitment to engaging with the exercises and lessons presented in this workbook is a testament to your resilience and determination to live your best life.

As you reflect on your experiences and insights gained from this workbook, I encourage you to celebrate your progress and achievements. Each exercise completed, each lesson learned, and each moment of self-discovery is a significant step forward on your path to personal transformation.

Thank you for your openness, your curiosity, and your commitment to your own growth and well-being. May the wisdom and insights gained from "The Silva Mind Control Method" continue to guide and inspire you on your journey to living a life of purpose, fulfillment, and empowerment.

With deepest appreciation and warmest regards,

Michelle Danatwa Publishing

END OF WORKBOOK

Manufactured by Amazon.ca
Acheson, AB